BRAZIL

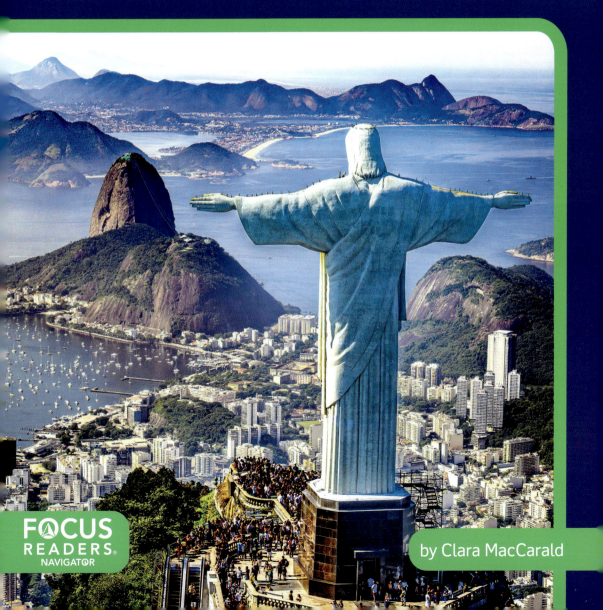

by Clara MacCarald

FOCUS READERS®
NAVIGATOR

WWW.FOCUSREADERS.COM

Focus Readers is distributed by North Star Editions:
sales@northstareditions.com | 888-417-0195

Produced for Focus Readers by Red Line Editorial.

Content Consultant: Seth W. Garfield, PhD, Professor of Brazilian History, The University of Texas at Austin

Photographs ©: Mischa Schoemaker/DPPA/Sipa USA/AP Images, cover, 1; Shutterstock Images, 4–5, 14–15, 17, 19, 20–21, 23, 24, 26–27, 28; Red Line Editorial, 6; Anderson Coelho/Getty Images, 8–9; Ettore Chiereguini/AGIF/AP Images, 11; Greg Gibson/AP Images, 13

Library of Congress Cataloging-in-Publication Data
Names: MacCarald, Clara, 1979- author.
Title: Brazil / by Clara MacCarald.
Description: Mendota Heights, MN : Focus Readers, [2025] | Series: Countries | Includes index. | Audience: Grades 4-6
Identifiers: LCCN 2024023647 (print) | LCCN 2024023648 (ebook) | ISBN 9798889982180 (hardcover) | ISBN 9798889982746 (paperback) | ISBN 9798889983804 (pdf) | ISBN 9798889983309 (ebook)
Subjects: LCSH: Brazil--Juvenile literature.
Classification: LCC F2508.5 .M23 2025 (print) | LCC F2508.5 (ebook) | DDC 981--dc23/eng/20230522
LC record available at https://lccn.loc.gov/2024023647
LC ebook record available at https://lccn.loc.gov/2024023648

Printed in the United States of America
Mankato, MN
012025

ABOUT THE AUTHOR

Clara MacCarald is a freelance writer with a master's degree in ecology and natural resources. She lives with her family in an off-grid house nestled in the forests of central New York. When not parenting her daughter, she spends her time writing nonfiction books for kids.

TABLE OF CONTENTS

CHAPTER 1

WELCOME TO BRAZIL

Brazil is a huge country in South America. More than 218 million people live there. The citizens are diverse. Their ancestors came from many places. Some were native to Brazil. Some were settlers from Europe. Some came from Asia and the Middle East. Some were **enslaved** and brought from Africa.

The Cathedral of Brasília is a famous landmark in Brazil's capital city.

Brazil is the world's fifth-largest country. It features many different landscapes. The Atlantic Ocean borders Brazil to the north and east. Rio de Janeiro is a famous city on the coast. The city is known for its beauty. It has amazing mountains and beaches.

MAP OF BRAZIL

São Paulo is Brazil's largest city. More than 20 million people live there.

The Amazon Rainforest is in Brazil's northern region. The rainforest covers nearly half the country. It is the largest rainforest on Earth. The Amazon River flows through the rainforest. It is the world's largest river.

The Pantanal is in the western part of Brazil. This area is one of Earth's largest **wetlands**. Brazil also has highlands. These mountain areas cover much of the center and southeast. Brasília is a city in the highlands. It is Brazil's capital. The government carefully planned the building of Brasília.

CHAPTER 2

HISTORY

The area that is now Brazil has been home to **Indigenous** people for more than 11,000 years. Millions of Indigenous people formed different tribes and nations. Some hunted and gathered. Others built cities and roads. They farmed and gardened the land.

Indigenous peoples have relied on the Amazon River for thousands of years.

In 1500, a Portuguese explorer landed in Brazil. His name was Pedro Álvares Cabral. He claimed the area for Portugal. Soon, Portuguese **colonists** arrived. They brought enslaved Africans. The Portuguese also enslaved Indigenous people. A Christian group called the Jesuits came, too. They wanted Indigenous people to become Christian.

Europeans took over Indigenous land. They fought and killed many Indigenous people. Europeans brought deadly illnesses, too. Millions of Indigenous people died. The colonists kept moving west. Some of them looked for new land to settle. Some hoped to find gold

Dom Pedro I became the first emperor of Brazil in 1822.

or other riches. And some looked for more people to enslave or to turn into Christians.

In 1822, a major change came. The son of the Portuguese king broke away from Portugal. He announced that Brazil was independent. Brazil became an **empire**.

But in 1889, people overthrew the empire. Brazil became a **republic**.

In 1964, another upheaval happened. João Goulart was the president. Brazil's military thought he was too liberal. Many conservatives didn't like his policies. So, the military overthrew him. The United States backed the Brazilian military. That

SLAVERY IN BRAZIL

Colonists in Brazil enslaved millions of people. They made people grow sugarcane and mine gold and diamonds. Some people escaped. They created communities far from the rest of society. Many of these communities still exist. Brazil ended slavery in 1888. But its brutal history continues to affect Black and Indigenous communities.

Brazilian president Fernando Collor de Mello (right) meets with US president George H. W. Bush in 1991.

helped the military take control of the government. The military held power for 20 years. During this period, the government put many Brazilians in jail. It also tortured thousands of people.

In 1985, the military finally gave up power. The people elected a new president. He took office in 1989. Brazil became a republic once again.

CHAPTER 3

CLIMATE, PLANTS, AND ANIMALS

Brazil crosses the **equator**. So, most of the country has a warm climate. Water is plentiful. Brazilian waters are full of life. Humpback whales live in the ocean. Manatees live close to the coast. Some manatees live in rivers, too. Brazil also has river dolphins.

Approximately 10 million yacare caimans live in Brazil.

The Amazon River is full of wildlife. Pirarucu live there. These fish grow nearly 10 feet (3 m) long. Pirarucu are one of the largest freshwater fish.

The Amazon Rainforest is home to one-third of Earth's species. Big animals such as jaguars and monkeys live there. So do about 1,300 kinds of birds. The rainforest has hundreds of kinds of frogs and salamanders. It also has more than 10,000 kinds of beetle. Around 80,000 species of plants live in the rainforest, too. That includes Brazil nut trees, kapok trees, palms, and vines.

The Pantanal is also full of wildlife. The huge wetland has more than 320 fish

The jaguar is the biggest cat in the Americas. Nearly 90 percent of all jaguars live in the Amazon.

species and 650 bird species. Storks and spoonbills form giant flocks in the region. Giant anteaters and capybaras live there, too. The Pantanal is also home to green anacondas. They are Earth's biggest snake. Plants in the area include hyacinths and reeds.

HEAT AND GASES

Climate change is caused by high levels of greenhouse gases. These gases trap heat in Earth's **atmosphere**. People often release greenhouse gases when they burn coal or other fuels. Brazil produces more greenhouse gases than any other country in South America.

Forests help take greenhouse gases out of the atmosphere. But people are cutting and burning parts of the Amazon Rainforest. The damaged rainforest can't take in as much of the gases. And trees release greenhouse gases when they burn.

Climate change is making Brazil hotter and drier. In 2020, the Pantanal had less water than usual. Huge parts of the wetland burned. Many animals died. Low water also harms farms. Farmers grow far fewer crops.

People burn parts of the Amazon Rainforest to make room for farms. Other fires are natural.

And **dams** make less electricity. In 2023, heat waves hit Brazil. The hot weather was dangerous. Officials warned people not to exercise outside. They warned people about possible forest fires.

Brazil's government promised to reduce greenhouse gases. It also made a plan to protect the Amazon Rainforest. However, many scientists said the government must act faster.

CHAPTER 4

RESOURCES, ECONOMY, AND GOVERNMENT

Brazil is full of natural resources. For example, the country has huge amounts of water. Dams use flowing water to make electricity. Dams provide more than half of Brazil's power.

Mining is also important in Brazil. The country produces important minerals. These include gold, tin, and diamonds.

Itaipú Dam is one of the world's largest hydroelectric power plants.

Brazil leads Central and South America in oil production. Brazil also creates many products. It makes cars, planes, and electronics. Overall, Brazil has the ninth-largest economy in the world.

Farming is a major part of Brazil's economy. Brazil grows more coffee than any other country. Other important crops include oranges, soybeans, and corn. Farmers also raise livestock such as cows and chickens.

Brazil is a republic. The country is led by a president. Brazilians elect the president every four years. There are 26 states in Brazil. Each one has a state government.

In 2023, Luiz Inácio Lula da Silva began his third term as Brazil's president.

Brazil's national government has three branches. The first is the executive branch. This branch is led by the president. It carries out the laws. It also deals with other countries. The second branch is the legislative branch. It is known as the National Congress. The National Congress makes Brazil's laws.

 The Supreme Federal Court is the highest court in the judicial branch.

It also gives the president permission to start wars. The third branch is the judicial branch. Its courts make rulings when people disagree about what laws mean.

Brazil has a constitution. This is a written document. It states all the rights that people have. For example, the constitution says people have the right to free speech. It also talks about the land. It says Indigenous people have a right to their land. However, the government does not always protect the rights stated in the constitution.

ELECTION FIGHT

In 2022, President Jair Bolsonaro ran for re-election. He lost. Luiz Inácio Lula da Silva won. The vote was close. Bolsonaro refused to accept the results. Some Brazilians were angry. They wanted him to keep leading the country. In January 2023, a group of Bolsonaro's supporters attacked government buildings. Many were arrested. They failed to remove Lula from power.

CHAPTER 5

PEOPLE AND CULTURE

Brazil's people and culture are diverse. Most people speak Portuguese. But there are 274 Indigenous languages in the country. Other languages spoken in Brazil include Italian, German, Polish, and Japanese.

Many Brazilians are Christian. Other religions include Buddhism and Islam.

Brazilians in São Paulo celebrate a festival for the Queen of the Sea.

Indigenous Brazilians and others march against climate change at an event in Belgium in 2022.

People practice Judaism and Candomblé, too. Others don't practice a religion.

Many Brazilians consider themselves white. More than half consider themselves mixed race or Black. People and governments don't always treat Black and Indigenous Brazilians fairly. Their communities tend to be poorer.

In 2022, Brazil had nearly 1.7 million Indigenous people. These people belonged to more than 300 different groups. Some groups hold large pieces of land. Approximately half of Brazil's Indigenous people live in the Amazon region. All of these Indigenous groups add to Brazil's diverse culture.

BRAZILIAN CARNIVAL

Carnival is a holiday. It comes from the Catholic faith. People celebrate with music and parades. They dance in the streets and wear fancy clothes. The world's biggest Carnival happens in Rio de Janeiro. Millions of visitors come to watch and take part. Other Brazilian cities hold Carnival events, too.

FOCUS QUESTIONS

Write your answers on a separate piece of paper.

1. Write a paragraph describing the main ideas of Chapter 2.

2. What area of Brazil are you most interested in visiting? Why?

3. What is the Pantanal?
   - **A.** one of the largest cities in the world
   - **B.** one of the biggest wetlands in the world
   - **C.** one of the longest rivers in the world

4. Why might people want to cut down trees in the Amazon Rainforest?
   - **A.** to release more greenhouse gases
   - **B.** to get wood or clear land for farming
   - **C.** because nothing lives in the rainforest

Answer key on page 32.

GLOSSARY

atmosphere
The layers of gases that surround a planet, moon, or star.

climate change
A human-caused global crisis involving long-term changes in Earth's temperature and weather patterns.

colonists
People who move into an area and take control.

dams
Walls built across streams or rivers to hold back water.

empire
A group of nations or territories ruled by a powerful government.

enslaved
Forced to work without pay and owned as property.

equator
An imaginary line that runs around the middle of Earth.

Indigenous
Native to a region, or belonging to ancestors who lived in a region before colonists arrived.

republic
A country governed by elected leaders.

wetlands
Areas where the ground has a lot of water.

TO LEARN MORE

BOOKS

Dickmann, Nancy. *Your Passport to Brazil*. North Mankato, MN: Capstone Press, 2023.

Kerry, Isaac. *Spotlight on Brazil*. Minneapolis: Lerner Publications, 2024.

Van, R. L. *Brazil*. Minneapolis: Abdo Publishing, 2023.

NOTE TO EDUCATORS

Visit **www.focusreaders.com** to find lesson plans, activities, links, and other resources related to this title.

INDEX